DIGITAL AND INFORMATION LITERACY ™

# UNDERSTANDING THE WORLD OF
## USER-GENERATED CONTENT

EMILY POPEK

rosen publishing's
rosen
central®

New York

Published in 2011 by The Rosen Publishing Group, Inc.
29 East 21st Street, New York, NY 10010

**Library of Congress Cataloging-in-Publication Data**

Popek, Emily.
Understanding the world of user-generated content / Emily Popek.—1st ed.
     p. cm.—(Digital and information literacy)
Includes bibliographical references and index.
ISBN 978-1-4358-9431-0 (library binding)
ISBN 978-1-4488-0598-3 (pbk)
ISBN 978-1-4488-0601-0 (6-pack)
1. User-generated content—Juvenile literature. 2. Social media—Juvenile literature. 3. Web 2.0—Juvenile literature. I. Title.
ZA4482.P67 2011
006.7—dc22

                                                            2010003055

*Manufactured in the United States of America*

CPSIA Compliance Information: Batch #S10YA: For further information, contact Rosen Publishing, New York, New York, at 1-800-237-9932.

# CONTENTS

# INTRODUCTION

When the Internet first became available to a large number of people in the 1990s, it was often referred to as the "information superhighway." People were said to navigate from Web site to Web site the way a driver navigates from one place to another. Links from one Web site to another were described as being similar to streets connecting different locations.

Today's Internet users aren't just going from Web site to Web site and looking at what's there. Instead, they are actively participating in the Web by creating their own sites or blogs, sharing video and audio files online, helping shape the content of the sites they visit. In other words, people are creating what is known as user-generated content, or UGC.

Web applications that allow user participation are known as Web 2.0. A lot of user-generated content is text, but UGC comes in virtually every medium. Anyone who has ever posted a comment on a Web site, uploaded photos to share, or created a Facebook survey has generated content. A lot of UGC is created and shared just for fun. In fact, some of the Web's most popular sites, such as YouTube, are almost entirely made up of UGC. However, there are other types of UGC that can be useful for students doing research on a variety of different topics. The online encyclopedia Wikipedia is one of the Web's largest collections of UGC; it contains millions of entries created and edited by thousands of people from around the world.

This book will discuss what UGC and Web 2.0 are. It will show how they can be useful for research and how to evaluate these sources to make sure they are reliable and appropriate for research purposes. Finally, it will show students how they can participate in Web 2.0 by creating Web sites, podcasts, or other projects.

# Chapter 1

# What Is Web 2.0?

n his book *Research Strategies*, author William Badke defines Web 2.0 as "a concept, rather than a defined area of the Internet." He says that "if you imagine the average Web page to be a publication, a one-way communication from the author to the reader, Web 2.0 forms those parts of the World Wide Web that are interactive. We can include here blogs, wikis, RSS feeds, social networking sites, forums, chat, messaging, e-mail, and so on."

## The Prevalence of UGC

Many people are already familiar with Web sites such as Facebook and technologies like text messaging. People use Facebook and send texts to communicate with friends. However, these technologies can also be used for other purposes. Facebook users can become "fans" of *Time* magazine, CNN, or the *New York Times* to get news updates and swap comments with other people. Government agencies use

The social networking Web site Facebook (http://www.facebook.com), seen here on a mobile phone, contains many examples of user-generated content (UGC). Most content on Facebook comes from the people who use the site, not from the site's creators.

text messages to let people know about emergencies, roadwork, or storm warnings.

Most Web sites today are not user-generated. Instead, they are created and maintained by individuals or teams of people who work together. School Web sites, for example, are usually maintained by people who are responsible for updating the site. School officials, like principals and superintendents, trust that these people will do a good job of making sure the Web site is accurate and up-to-date.

---

File     Edit     View     Favorites     Tools     Help

THE ORIGIN OF WEB 2.0

## The Origin of Web 2.0

Web 2.0 is an expression that describes a new, interactive way of thinking about computers and the Internet. The number "2.0" refers to a new version of a previously existing product. In the past, when new versions of computer programs were introduced, they were often given a number. Whole numbers, like 2.0, usually referred to completely new versions of the computer program. If only some slight changes had been made, a decimal might be used to represent those changes. A computer program might go through versions 1.2, 1.4, 1.6, and 1.8—all with only slight modifications—before version 2.0 was released. Thus calling something 2.0 signifies that it is substantially different from the original.

The expression "Web 2.0" was first used in 1999 in an article titled "Fragmented Future" by Darcy DiNucci. DiNucci used the terms "1.0" and "2.0" to make the point that the Internet is always changing. She called the Internet of 1999 an "embryo" and a "prototype," and predicted that Web-capable software would soon be found on cell phones, handheld video game systems, and other devices.

If a school's Web site could be updated by just anyone, the principal might be a little nervous. Students could go to the Web site and write whatever they wanted. So could teachers, parents, or anyone else who wanted to express their opinion about the school. School officials might not want everybody to have equal control over the school's official Web site. Businesses, local governments, and many other groups feel the same way about their Web sites.

For a long time, virtually all Web sites were set up this way. Certain people controlled what was on the site, and no one else could change it— they could just look at it. Web 2.0 sites are different. People visiting Web 2.0 sites can post comments, change information, upload videos or photos, or do other things to contribute to the site itself.

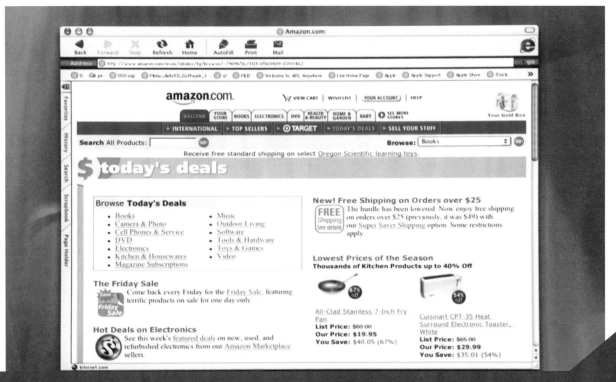

Web sites such as Amazon.com (http://www.amazon.com) feature a great deal of UGC, such as user reviews and ratings. Users can also create lists featuring their favorite music, books, or products.

# The Spread of Web 2.0

Blogs and Wikipedia are two familiar places to find UGC. But as Web 2.0 becomes more and more widespread, UGC is popping up on many different types of Web sites. UGC can be found on many newspaper Web

These Montana high school students are working together to produce an online magazine in their journalism class. As part of their class work, the students learn to create journalistic podcasts and content for Facebook, MySpace, and Twitter.

sites, where readers can post comments about news stories. It can be found on Web sites for companies like Amazon.com, Best Buy, and Target, where customers can leave feedback or ratings of products they have purchased. It can also be found on sites where users can post questions that are answered by other users.

Some Web sites monitor comments and make sure no one says anything inappropriate. If someone posts something offensive or libelous, the person monitoring the comments can remove the post. Some Web sites will even ban users from posting if they break the rules too many times.

Other Web sites have filters to prevent inappropriate comments from being posted in the first place. They might have software that checks each post for certain words, such as profanity or offensive language. Many Web sites also have safeguards to make sure that comments are relevant and appropriate to the topic.

Evaluating the accuracy or legitimacy of user-generated content can be challenging. Because just about anyone can post a comment, start a blog, record a podcast, or contribute to a wiki, it can be very hard to tell if information is truthful, accurate, and appropriate. By learning more about these information sources and how to evaluate them, students can decide how to incorporate Web 2.0 into their research. Since Web 2.0 is all about interactivity, many of these tools allow for hands-on learning as well as traditional research. Web 2.0 platforms such as photo-sharing, blogging, and document-sharing Web sites can also help students create projects beyond the traditional research paper or essay.

# Chapter 2

# From Encyclopedia to Wikipedia

**M**ore than 150 years ago, two Frenchmen, Denis Diderot and Jean d'Alembert, were hired to translate an English encyclopedia into French. Diderot was not satisfied with the book, so he began adding his own ideas to it.

Although Diderot's ideas, which challenged the government and the Catholic church, were controversial at the time, he is now considered the father of the modern encyclopedia. Diderot's *Encyclopédie* gathered information from many different people, and his goal was to make this information available to everyone.

In 2001, Jimmy Wales founded the Web site Wikipedia. This online encyclopedia, like Diderot's *Encyclopédie*, has also been called controversial and revolutionary, but for different reasons.

All encyclopedias have more than one author, but Wikipedia has more authors than any encyclopedia to date. Instead of being written by experts selected by an editor, Wikipedia's articles can be written and edited by anyone using the Internet.

Jimmy Wales, founder of the Web site Wikipedia, has been praised for the innovative idea of creating an entirely user-generated encyclopedia. The site remains controversial, however, as many people have criticized it for containing false or inaccurate information.

The name "Wikipedia" combines the Hawaiian word *wiki*, which means "fast," with the suffix "-pedia," as in "encyclopedia." A man named Ward Cunningham used the word "wiki" for a computer database he created that could be edited and changed very quickly and easily. People from all over could log on to Cunningham's database to learn about computers, while also being able to contribute their own knowledge. Cunningham called it the WikiWikiWeb. Users were allowed to change not only things they had written, but things written by other people as well.

Wikipedia founder Jimmy Wales took the idea of a wiki—a collection of information that anyone can add to and edit—and expanded it beyond Cunningham's idea. Wales's Web site wasn't limited by subject. At the time of this writing, Wikipedia has more than thirteen million articles. These articles change all the time, as millions of people add information or revise existing information.

## Who Controls Wikipedia?

Books, magazines, and newspapers are carefully edited and fact-checked by editors and publishers. The author's and publisher's names are right there in the book for all to see. On the Web, it's not always so easy to figure out where the information comes from.

Many people have criticized Wikipedia for this. Since it's possible for anyone to add, change, or remove information from Wikipedia, there is no way to be sure the information is really accurate. According to Jimmy Wales and the people who work on Wikipedia, mistakes or false information will always be corrected eventually. Wales believes that more people are interested in correcting errors than playing pranks. By giving everyone equal access to Wikipedia, Wales hopes that the Web site will end up having the best possible information, based on knowledge collected and refined from millions of people.

So how can a reader tell if a Wikipedia entry is accurate? It's not always easy, but there are a lot of tools that can help. The first thing to look for are notes or advisories at the top of each Wikipedia entry. For example, an entry might show a symbol of an open book with a question mark on it, with a note that reads, "This article needs additional citations for verification." Citations show where the information in an entry comes from. These citations usually appear as footnotes.

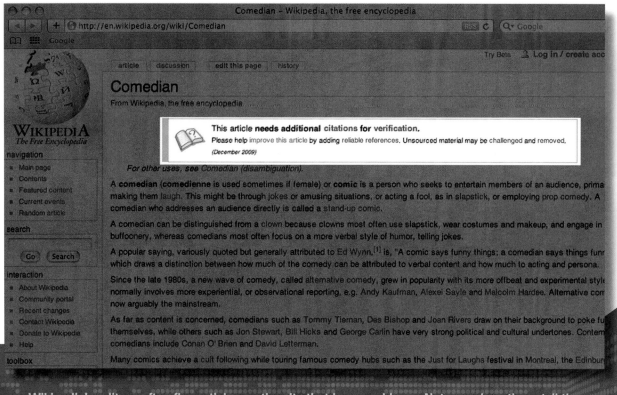

Wikipedia's editors often flag articles on the site that have problems. Notes such as these tell the reader if the article lacks citations, if the writing is unclear, or if the author seems to be biased.

The footnotes in a Wikipedia article might contain citations for articles in magazines like *Time*, scholarly books, or newspapers like the *New York Times*. Footnotes might also point to Web sites, blogs, or even radio or television programs. Wikipedia editors sometimes put notes on the Web site's articles to warn readers that the article might need improvement or be lacking in some way. One symbol is a broom, with a message saying, "This article may require cleanup to meet Wikipedia's quality standards." Wikipedia's "Cleanup" page explains that this means the article may have poor grammar, spelling, or punctuation; it may be inaccurate, or lacking in sources; or it may not be sufficiently neutral or unbiased.

File    Edit    View    Favorites    Tools    Help

FOOTNOTES AND ENDNOTES

## Footnotes and Endnotes

A footnote is a numbered citation found at the bottom of a page. The first footnote in a book, or on a Web site, will be marked with a very small "1" at the end of a word or sentence. This number indicates where to look in the list of notes at the bottom of the page. Footnotes often contain references, or additional information pertaining to a particular sentence or idea in the text. When notes are grouped at the end of the book, they are called endnotes. Students writing research papers may be asked to use footnotes or endnotes to explain where their information came from.

According to Wikipedia, the Web site tries to follow the example of traditional encyclopedias and other reference materials by presenting neutral, unbiased information on each subject. This means that each Wikipedia entry should be based on facts that can be proved or agreed upon and should include multiple points of view.

## Opinion and Bias

It's important to look out for people's personal opinions when researching a topic. For instance, statements like, "Apples are stupid," or "Nobody really likes to eat apples," are examples of opinions, not objective facts. The first statement, "Apples are stupid," represents how a person feels about apples—not a fact about apples themselves. The second statement, "Nobody really likes to eat apples," can't be proved. It would be easy to disprove this statement by asking a few people if they, or anyone they know, like to eat apples. Both these statements are opinions, rather than facts. An article containing statements such as these may be trying to express a certain viewpoint, rather than just provide facts about the subject.

Statements that are generalizations, such as "People like to eat cheese," or statements of opinion like, "Macintosh computers are better than PCs," may point to a source's bias. Unless general statements are explained with statistics, facts, data, or other credible information, these may be clues that you are reading a biased source.

The ability to distinguish biased sources from unbiased sources when conducting research is an important skill to learn. An unbiased or neutral article about President Barack Obama should include information about all aspects of his presidency—things he has done that were popular and things that some people did not agree with. That way, readers can decide for themselves if they agree or disagree with the president's decisions. An article that presents only one side of an argument shouldn't be the only source used. It should be balanced by other sources that present opposing viewpoints. Even though Wikipedia's editors try to make sure that all entries are accurate and neutral, students still need to use their best judgment when reading Wikipedia.

It's not always easy to determine if a source is biased. In her book *The Internet Playground*, Ellen Seiter looks at young people using the Internet for research. She says that "it takes a great deal of sophistication to judge online information. . . Advanced critical thinking skills are necessary to sort out good and bad information on the Web."

Seiter wrote about a group of young students who were looking for information about the construction of a new baseball stadium for the San Diego Padres. Many students found articles from a local paper reprinted on the Padres' official Web site and were eager to use the articles in their research. As Seiter points out, however, the Padres were careful to include only news articles that were favorable to the stadium, excluding any criticisms.

"Not one of them suspected that stories printed on the Padres' official Web site could be slanted toward one side of the ballpark story . . . Indeed

Newspaper Web sites, such as the *New York Times* site, are generally good places to research current events. Students must remember, however, that newspapers contain editorials as well as news reporting and that even the news may be biased toward a certain viewpoint.

this polished, highly truncated version of local events seemed to answer all of their questions," Seiter says.

Seiter's story is a reminder that, even when a source is legitimate and truthful, it may still only be telling one side of the story.

# TEN GREAT QUESTIONS

## TO ASK A LIBRARIAN

1. How can I find out who the author of this Web site is?

2. How can I contact the author of an article or Web site?

3. Am I allowed to access Web sites that are blocked by the library?

4. Does the library have subscriptions to any news or research databases?

5. How can I tell if this Web site contains credible information?

6. How can I create my own podcast?

7. Where can I find trustworthy blogs, videos, or podcasts related to my research topic?

8. How can I tell if a Web site is trustworthy?

9. How can I find another point of view on this topic?

10. What Web sites featuring UGC do you recommend for research?

## Chapter 3

# Blogs

There are forms of UGC that have been around a lot longer than the Internet. During early U.S. history, people used broadsides—large sheets of paper, printed only on one side—to express their opinions about political, social, or other matters. Today, blogs allow people to do the same thing. Broadsides and blogs have a lot in common. First, they are both democratic. Broadsides could be published by just about anyone, whether they were rich or poor, educated or not. Similarly, anyone can post comments on Web sites or have their own blog.

Second, both allow people to hide their real identity. Broadsides could be published completely anonymously so that no one would ever know who wrote them. While many Web sites ask users to log in with a user name, there is little to prevent someone from signing a false name to his or her profile.

Third, UGC is not always subject to the same rigorous examination as other published material. Statements of fact or opinion can often be made more freely in these forums than in traditional media, such as books, magazines, and newspapers. Bloggers don't need anyone else—like a publisher or an editor—to agree with their opinion to get it out there.

This was also true for the writers of broadsides, who often expressed controversial opinions or could not find a newspaper to publish their writing. By printing a broadside, these writers were able to directly reach their audience.

## Sharing Information

When blogs first started, many of them were like diaries, where people would write about their lives or give their opinions. Today, journalists, celebrities, scientists, politicians, and other public figures write blogs. Companies use blogs to share information about their products. Writers, musicians, and athletes use

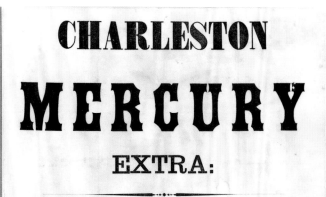
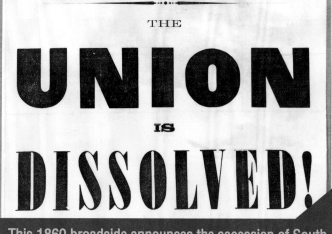

CHARLESTON
MERCURY
EXTRA:

Passed unanimously at 1.15 o'clock, P. M., December 20th, 1860.

AN ORDINANCE

To dissolve the Union between the State of South Carolina and other States united with her under the compact entitled "The Constitution of the United States of America."

We, the People of the State of South Carolina, in Convention assembled, do declare and ordain, and it is hereby declared and ordained,

That the Ordinance adopted by us in Convention, on the twenty-third day of May, in the year of our Lord one thousand seven hundred and eighty-eight, whereby the Constitution of the United States of America was ratified, and also, all Acts and parts of Acts of the General Assembly of this State, ratifying amendments of the said Constitution, are hereby repealed; and that the union now subsisting between South Carolina and other States, under the name of "The United States of America," is hereby dissolved.

THE
UNION
IS
DISSOLVED!

This 1860 broadside announces the secession of South Carolina from the United States. Today, breaking news updates can be found on blogs or on Twitter.

blogs to communicate with their fans. Even the White House has a blog.

Why are there so many blogs out there? For one thing, updating blogs with new information is usually easier than updating other types of Web pages. There are a lot of Web sites that allow anyone to sign up and create a blog just by clicking a few buttons. The layout and appearance of the blog can be chosen from several different options. Once a person is signed up, all he or she has to do is sign in to the blog and start typing. Saved posts are added to the blog, with all the fonts, colors, and other tools the user had already selected.

Before blog software became available, most Web sites had to be designed from scratch. This could usually only be accomplished by someone who was knowledgeable in computer and Web programming. Changes to the Web site often meant a lot of work for the programmer, who had to change the code that made the Web site look and work the way it did.

Blogs are a quick and easy way to not only reach an audience, but also to interact with it. For instance,

News organizations such as CNN use blogs as a quick, informal way to communicate with readers. The blog format, which usually lists the most current information at the top of the screen, makes it easy for readers to see what's new.

Lee Welles, author of the young-adult book series Gaia Girls, posts contests, challenges, and videos on her blog to keep in touch with readers. The television news channel CNN invites viewers to comment on its blog and often reads these comments on the air to show how different people feel about an issue.

Most blogging Web sites make it easy to include videos, music, photos, and other documents. Music groups like the Jonas Brothers can post new songs and videos on their blog. Movie companies can post trailers for their upcoming films or interviews with actors. Politicians can use blogs to share videos of their speeches and public appearances.

## Using Blogs as a Resource

Depending on the topic being researched, blogs could be a big help, or no help at all. Blogs are often the quickest places to get breaking news about current events, and some blogs provide real-time updates about ongoing events. Blogs are also a good place to find links to a

Journalists such as Christiane Amanpour of the CNN television network interact with viewers through blogs. The "Amanpour" blog features behind-the-scenes commentary from Amanpour and the staff that work on the journalist's interview program, as well as exclusive webcasts.

lot of different sources on a particular topic. Students should check with their teacher or librarian to see if a particular blog is an appropriate source for research.

Students researching geography, history, or science projects might not find blogs to be helpful. These subjects aren't as likely to change much with current events. Books at a school or public library will probably have more information on these subjects than a blog. However, blogs with credible information can be useful for tracking changes as they happen. For instance, blogs can be very helpful when it comes to keeping abreast of current political events. There are also many blogs dedicated to tracking scientific and technological innovations, particularly in fields like computers, energy, and medicine.

File    Edit    View    Favorites    Tools    Help

CONTENT FILTERS

## Content Filters

Many print and online publications have strict rules about what they will publish. Respected magazines like *Time*, *Newsweek*, and *National Geographic* usually do not allow profanity and adult language to appear in their articles. Many publications do not have the same policies regarding language, however. Someone's personal blog posts might contain profanity or other content that is inappropriate for young people. Even if an online publication has strict standards about language and content, people might post comments that violate these standards.

The computers in junior high and high school libraries sometimes have software that filters out inappropriate content. Unfortunately, these filters aren't always effective. Students should always check with a teacher, parent, or librarian before visiting an unfamiliar Web site to make sure it's appropriate.

Just as with Wikipedia, it's important to evaluate blogs based on where the information is coming from. Official blogs, like the ones found on the White House Web site, are different from someone's personal blog. Official blogs are monitored by the organization responsible for the Web site. Blogs like these, which are linked to a company or organization you can trust, can be good places to look for news and ideas.

Many national newspapers or magazines have blogs on their Web sites. These are good places to research local issues, but it's important to look carefully at who's writing them. If the author of the blog doesn't work for the newspaper, the blog might not be subjected to rigorous editing and fact-checking. If the author of the blog is someone who works for a national newspaper or magazine, there's a better chance that the blog has been

Barack Obama was the first U.S. president to add a blog to the White House Web site (http://www.whitehouse.gov). "The White House" blog features weekly Web addresses from the president, as well as news and commentary from White House staffers.

looked over by an editor. "Citizen journalists" may present some interesting ideas and information, but they might only tell one side of the story. Their viewpoints should be balanced with other sources.

Students who find interesting information on a newspaper's Web site may even be able to contact the blogger to learn more. Students can ask their teacher for permission to send an e-mail, submit a comment on the blog to request more information, or to ask for an interview with the author.

Personal blogs are different from blogs that are associated with a certain company or organization. Sometimes the author's name, picture, and even e-mail address will be listed on a personal blog; sometimes there won't be any information at all about who's writing it. Once again, student researchers have to be detectives and try to figure out who is responsible for the Web site's content.

## Evaluating the Information on a Blog

Imagine a student is doing research about President Barack Obama and finds a blog called "Tom's Thoughts." This blog has a lot of entries about the president and the things he has done while in office, but the student is not sure if the blog is an unbiased source.

The student can start doing detective work by looking for a profile of the blogger. The link to this profile might be called "About Me," "About Tom's Thoughts," or something similar. Many blogs contain short descriptions like this so that people know what the blog is about. These descriptions are not unlike the brief author biographies found in the back of books. If the student reads that the author of "Tom's Thoughts" belongs to a group called Don't Reelect Barack Obama, this will be a clue that the blog is not an impartial, unbiased Web site. While the blog may contain much interesting information, it probably isn't a good source of facts. The same would be true if the student found a blog that only praised the president and defended all his decisions. Neither of these blogs would be neutral, unbiased sources of information—but they might be great sources for different people's opinions.

Students doing online research have to use critical thinking skills to evaluate the UGC they find. They must be prepared to do some detective work to find out who the author of a blog is and how reliable a blogger might be as a source of information.

Writers who are trying to convince the reader about something only include information supporting their opinion.

If there is no profile section on the blog, the student can do an Internet search to see if any other Web sites mention "Tom's Thoughts." Some blogs draw thousands or even millions of readers and are considered very influential. Others are read by only a handful of people. If a credible source, such as *Time* magazine or the *Wall Street Journal*, calls "Tom's Thoughts" "one of the foremost conservative blogs," it may be a very good source for research about different political viewpoints. On the other hand, if the student cannot find any mention of it among major news sources, it may not be the best source for his or her research.

# MYTHS & FACTS

**MYTH** Wikipedia entries can't be trusted.

**FACT** Since articles on Wikipedia are always changing, it's hard to generalize about the Web site's accuracy. Some studies have shown that Wikipedia can be about as accurate as traditional scholarly sources. In 2005, the science journal *Nature* did a side-by-side comparison of Wikipedia entries and *Encyclopaedia Britannica* entries on several different scientific subjects. They found the two sources to be about equally accurate. Still, information found on Wikipedia should be checked against a credible source, such as a trusted book or newspaper. Attitudes about Wikipedia are still evolving as the number of contributors to the site grows.

**MYTH** Blogs are just for people who want to rant and rave about a certain topic.

**FACT** While many blogs feature opinions or personal information, that's not all blogs can be used for. Many offer up-to-date news that rivals anything found in major newspapers. Other blogs are collaborations between numerous authors, offering a variety of different viewpoints or ideas.

**MYTH** There are no informative or useful videos on YouTube.

**FACT** YouTube has thousands of videos devoted to academic topics such as history, science, fine art, and more. Many of these can be found on YouTube EDU, a channel featuring videos prepared by colleges across the country.

# Chapter 4

# Branching Out on the Web

ne of the things that makes Web 2.0 so special is the opportunities it offers for interactivity. It's one thing to read a blog or watch a video online, but actually creating a blog or uploading a video is what Web 2.0 is all about. This chapter will look at how Web 2.0 can be the platform for many different types of projects, in addition to serving as a research tool. However, students who want to post content online—whether it's a podcast, a video, or a blog—should check with their teacher first.

## Podcasts

One of the most exciting tools Web 2.0 offers is podcasting. The word "podcast" is a combination of "iPod" and "broadcast." It was created in 2004 by the writer Ben Hammersley to describe digital recordings found online that could be downloaded to personal audio players, like iPods. Podcasts can also be played on a computer.

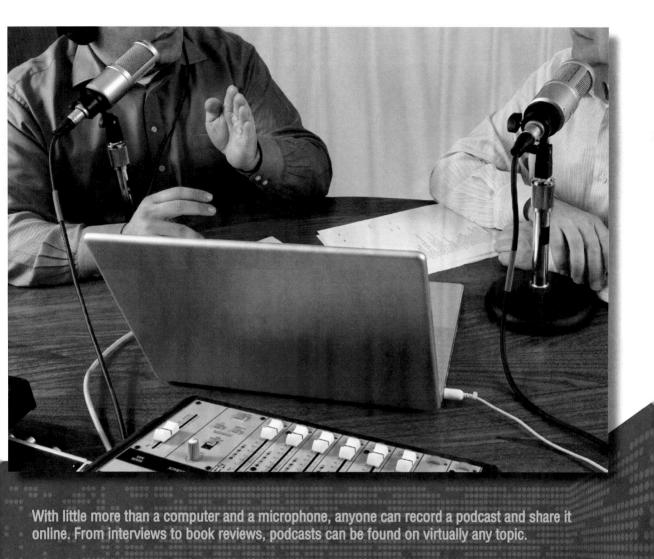

With little more than a computer and a microphone, anyone can record a podcast and share it online. From interviews to book reviews, podcasts can be found on virtually any topic.

Just like blogs, podcasts can be found on virtually every subject imaginable. Many podcasts are similar to radio news broadcasts, with one or more people talking about issues and ideas. Some are like diaries or journals, while others are sophisticated, fully formed programs, with music, sound effects, and more.

The White House Web site (http://www.whitehouse.gov) features the blogs of various government agencies and councils. This blog post was written by the chairperson of the Council on Environmental Quality.

The same way that blogs allow virtually anyone to get their ideas out in writing, podcasts allow people to essentially create and broadcast their own radio programs. What makes podcasting so exciting is that these programs can be created very easily, without the expensive recording and broadcasting equipment used by radio stations. Many students around the world are already creating their own podcasts, from college students down to elementary school classes.

According to Terry Burrows, author of *Blogs, Wikis, MySpace, and More*, one of the things that sets podcasts apart from other audio files online is that many people subscribe to certain podcasts, just like you might subscribe to a magazine. When a new podcast becomes available, the audio file is automatically downloaded to subscribers. Not all podcasts are broadcast to subscribers on a regular schedule, but many of them are.

Just as with blogging, there are a lot of Web sites and software applications available to help people listen to podcasts and create their own. Apple's digital media player iTunes features thousands of podcasts that subscribers can download from its Web site. Free software programs like Juice can be downloaded and used to browse through thousands of podcasts. Web sites like Podbean offer a place for podcasters to upload and list their own podcasts. The Education Podcast Network offers information and directories specific to educational podcasts, from elementary school through college. This site is a good example of a starting point for students who want to create a podcast or learn more about using podcasts in the classroom.

## Video Sharing

Video-sharing sites like YouTube are Web 2.0's version of television. While a lot of the videos on YouTube are meant to be funny and entertaining, more and more people are using this free video-sharing site to educate and inform viewers. For instance, the White House has used YouTube videos to speak directly to the American people, just as previous administrations have

Washington high school student Javier Caceres directed a music video starring his classmates for a school project that has since become a hit on YouTube. Web sites like YouTube allow users to share their content with thousands of viewers.

used television or radio addresses. Teachers and college professors post educational videos on YouTube; in fact, there is even a separate site called TeacherTube that focuses just on educational materials.

Creating a video for a school assignment can be a lot of fun, but students should make sure to talk to their teacher to see if this would be appropriate for the project at hand. In addition, students should be aware that material posted to video-sharing Web sites might be protected by copyright law. Copyrighted material should not be duplicated or reproduced without permission

# Blogging

Just like podcasts and video-sharing Web sites, blogs can not only help students conduct research, but also be a way for students to showcase what they've learned, or engage in a hands-on learning experience.

There are a number of situations in which it might make sense for students to start their own blog at school. Students could create their own school newspaper or literary magazine in the form of a blog. Traditional newspaper and magazine publishing can be expensive and time-consuming. A school news blog, or creative writing blog, could be created at no cost using free blogging software. Students who want to start an online newspaper or literary magazine should consider asking a teacher to serve as their adviser. Advisers can help students get permission to set up a blog and help the students decide what type of stories or content should be included.

A blog could also be used to collaborate on a creative writing project or to share ideas with students from other classrooms or even other schools. By giving many different people access to the same blog, different students could log in to add their own thoughts and ideas to a news story, a school report, or any other creative project. With a teacher's permission, students could also create personal essays, journals, or similar projects in blog form, rather than on paper.

## Online Educational Videos

Because some YouTube videos are not appropriate for students to watch in school, many schools block the site from their computers. Similar sites that offer educational content, such as TeacherTube, SchoolTube, and doFlick may be permitted because these sites offer more protection against inappropriate content.

Students who find that they are unable to access video-sharing Web sites can speak with their teacher, librarian, or media center supervisor to find out if the sites can be unlocked. There are many video-sharing Web sites out there, including ones that are designed specifically for schools. In most cases, students should be able to find a site that will be appropriate and allowed for use in school, whether it's to watch videos or post some of their own.

## Conclusion

The information available on the Internet is virtually endless. In a way, this is a wonderful thing because it means that anyone who goes online can learn about anything they want. At the same time, having so much information at one's fingertips can also be confusing and overwhelming. It's tough to know where to start or how to sort through everything to pick the good from the bad.

Learning how to sort out what information is useful from what isn't can help students develop their critical thinking skills. Students who can pick out a blog that's balanced and unbiased, among the many that aren't, are learning how to evaluate sources and ask questions about both sides of the story. Students who can find educational, informative, and relevant videos

With support from teachers, students can develop their creativity by making their own blogs, podcasts, or videos, and develop their critical thinking skills by using these resources for research.

on YouTube are learning to concentrate and focus on the task at hand instead of getting sidetracked. These skills will be useful beyond just the scope of one or two research projects: they will help students in any kind of future academic pursuit. The world of Web 2.0 and UGC is just as vast and full of distractions as the real world. As students navigate the real world, just as when they navigate the Web, they will benefit from knowing how to evaluate the trustworthiness, accuracy, and appropriateness of the information around them.

# GLOSSARY

**audio** Related to sound or hearing. Audio files, such as MP3s, only contain sound.

**biased** Predisposed to a certain point of view; not open-minded.

**blog** A shortened version of Weblog. Blogs are online documents that are updated frequently with new content.

**broadside** Broadsides were one-page documents published to express political or other views, often anonymously.

**collaborate** To work together on a project.

**content** Text, images, video, or audio data.

**copyright** Legal protection for written or recorded content.

**database** A collection of data in an organized structure.

**fact** Something that can be verified, or proved to be true.

**libel** False statements about someone.

**opinion** A personal belief, judgment, or impression; something that cannot be proved.

**platform** A structure or base. In terms of computers, a system within which a computer program operates.

**podcast** An audio file distributed via the Internet.

**post** To create or upload something to a Web site.

**software** Computer programs or applications.

**streaming** Content, such as an audio or video file, that is delivered continuously while it is being viewed or heard by the user.

**upload** To transfer a file from a local host computer to a remote computer or server. It is the opposite of downloading.

**user** A person who uses a particular product or service.

**Web 2.0** Web sites or other Internet-capable media that allow for user interactivity.

Center for Media Literacy
23852 Pacific Coast Highway, #472
Malibu, CA 90265
(310) 456-1225
Web site: http://www.medialit.org
The Center for Media Literacy promotes and supports media literacy education. It works to help all citizens, especially young people, develop
critical thinking and media production skills.

KidsBeSafeOnline
P.O. Box 106
Cottleville, MO 63338
(636) 487-4290
Web site: http://www.kidsbesafeonline.com
KidsBeSafeOnline provides information for parents, teachers, and kids about
safe Web surfing.

Kid Witness News
One Panasonic Way, 3C-7
Secaucus, NJ 07094
Web site: http://www.panasonic.com/MECA/kwn
Kid Witness News is a program of the Panasonic corporation that teaches
young people how to film and produce their own videos. The organization's Web site has information about how schools can get involved in
the program, as well as tips and guidelines for anyone who wants to
create a video.

Library and Archives Canada
395 Wellington Street

Ottawa, ON K1A 0N4
Canada
(866) 578-7777
Web site: http://www.collectionscanada.gc.ca
Library and Archives Canada, an agency of the Canadian government,
    features an online learning center with research tools for students,
    teachers, and parents, including primary source documents.

Media Awareness Network
1500 Merivale Road, 3rd floor
Ottawa, ON K2E 6Z5
Canada
(800) 896-3342
Web site: http://www.media-awareness.ca
The Media Awareness Network is a nonprofit organization that provides
    information about young people and the media, including the Internet.

## Web Sites

Due to the changing nature of Internet links, Rosen Publishing has developed
an online list of Web sites related to the subject of this book. This site is
updated regularly. Please use this link to access the list:

http://www.rosenlinks.com/dil/ugc

# FOR FURTHER READING

Ayers, Phoebe, Charles Matthews, and Ben Yates. *How Wikipedia Works: And How You Can Be a Part of It*. San Francisco, CA: No Starch Press, 2008.

Badke, William. *Research Strategies: Finding Your Way Through the Information Fog*. Bloomington, IN: iUniverse, 2008.

Barret, Colin. *Digital Video for Beginners: A Step-by-Step Guide to Making Great Home Movies*. Asheville, NC: Lark Books, 2005.

Bell, Ann. *Exploring Web 2.0: Second Generation Interactive Tools–Blogs, Podcasts, Wikis, Networking, Virtual Words, and More*. Scotts Valley, CA: CreateSpace, 2009.

Burrows, Terry. *Blogs, Wikis, MySpace, and More: Everything You Want to Know About Using Web 2.0 but Are Afraid to Ask*. Chicago, IL: Chicago Review Press, 2008.

Castro, Elizabeth. *Publishing a Blog with Blogger: Visual QuickProject Guide*. Berkeley, CA: Peachpit Press, 2009.

Clegg, Brian. *Studying Using the Web: The Student's Guide to Using the Ultimate Information Resource*. New York, NY: Routledge, 2006.

Cochrane, Todd. *Podcasting: The Do-It-Yourself Guide*. Indianapolis, IN: Wiley Publishing, 2005.

Farkas, Bart. *Secrets of Podcasting*. Berkeley, CA: Peachpit Press, 2006.

Friedman, Lauri S. *The Internet*. Farmington Hills, MI: Greenhaven Press, 2007.

Gaines, Ann. *Ace Your Internet Research*. Berkeley Heights, NJ: Enslow Publishers, 2009.

Jakubiak, David J. *A Smart Kid's Guide to Doing Internet Research*. New York, NY: PowerKids Press, 2009.

Lowen, Nancy. *Just the Facts: Writing Your Own Research Report*. Mankato, MN: Picture Window Books, 2009.

Miller, Michael. *YouTube 4 You*. Ontario, Canada: Que, 2007.

Osborn, Jennifer, Benjamin Selfridge, and Peter Selfridge. *A Teen's Guide to Creating Web Pages and Blogs*. Waco, TX: Prufrock Press, 2008.

Pascaretti, Vicki, and Sara Wilkie. *Super Smart Information Strategies: Team Up Online*. Ann Arbor, MI: Cherry Lake Publishing, 2010.

Piontek, Jeffrey. *Blogs, Wikis, and Podcasts, Oh My! Electronic Media in the Classroom*. Huntington Beach, CA: Shell Education, 2009.

Richardson, Will. *Blogs, Wikis, Podcasts, and Other Powerful Web Tools for Classrooms*. Thousand Oaks, CA: Corwin Press, 2009.

Rosner, Marc Alan. *Science Fair Success Using the Internet*. Berkeley Heights, NJ: Enslow Publishers, 2006.

Stebbins, Leslie. *Student Guide to Research in the Digital Age: How to Locate and Evaluate Information Sources*. Santa Barbara, CA: Libraries Unlimited, 2005.

Taylor, Paige. *Consider the Source: Finding Reliable Information on the Internet*. Janesville, WI: Upstart Books, 2004.

Badke, William. *Research Strategies: Finding Your Way Through the Information Fog*. Bloomington, IN: iUniverse, 2008.

Dinucci, Darcy. "Fragmented Future." April 1999. Retrieved August 5, 2009 (http://www.cdinucci.com/Darcy2/articles/articlesindex.html).

Goodin, Dan. "Nature: 'Wikipedia Is Accurate'." Associated Press, December 14, 2005. Retrieved September 12, 2009 (http://www.usatoday.com/tech/news/2005-12-14-nature-wiki_x.htm).

Hammersley, Ben. "Audible Revolution." Guardian.co.uk, February 12, 2004. Retrieved August 5, 2009 (http://www.guardian.co.uk/media/2004/feb/12/broadcasting.digitalmedia).

Henninger, Maureen. *The Hidden Web*. Sydney, Australia: University of New South Wales Press, 2005.

HistoryWorld. "Biography of Denis Diderot." Retrieved August 8, 2009 (http://history-world.org/diderot.htm).

Lih, Andrew. *The Wikipedia Revolution: How a Bunch of Nobodies Created the World's Greatest Encyclopedia*. New York, NY: Hyperion, 2009.

Masters, Coco, et al. "It's a Wiki, Wiki, Wiki World." *Time*, May 29, 2005. Retrieved August 5, 2009 (http://www.time.com/time/magazine/article/0,9171,1066904-2,00.html).

Ostertag, Stephen, and Gaye Tuchman. "Blogs and News Processes: Net Neutrality and Digital Inequality." *Participation and Media Production: Critical Reflections on Content Creation*. Nico Carpentier and Benjamin De Cleen, eds. Newcastle, DE: Cambridge Scholars Publishing, 2008.

Seiter, Ellen. *The Internet Playground*. New York, NY: Peter Lang, 2005.

Tancer, Bill. *Click: What Millions of People Are Doing Online and Why It Matters*. New York, NY: Hyperion, 2008.

Tapscott, Don, and Anthony Williams. *Wikinomics: How Mass Collaboration Changes Everything*. New York, NY: Portfolio, 2006.

# INDEX

## About the Author

Emily Popek is a writer and an editor at the *Daily Star* newspaper in Oneonta, New York, where she checks the validity of sources, both online and off-line, on a daily basis.

## Photo Credits

Cover (top left), pp. 1 (top left), 29, 39 © www.istockphoto.com/René Mansi; cover (far right), p. 1 (far right) © www.istockphoto.com; cover (second from right), p. 1 (second from right), p. 33 © www.istockphoto.com/ Eliza Snow; cover (background), interior design © www.istockphoto.com; p. 7 Tony Avelar/Bloomberg via Getty Images; p. 9 © David Young-Wolff/ Photo Edit; p. 10 © AP Images; p. 13 Menahem Kahana/AFP/Getty Images; p. 18 © Karen Bleier/AFP/Getty Images; p. 21 The New York Public Library/Art Resouce, NY; pp. 22–23 Jupiter Images/Getty Images; pp. 24–25 Kaveh Kazemi/Getty Images; p. 36 Cliff DesPeaux/Seattle Times/MCT/Newscom.

Designer: Nicole Russo; Photo Researcher: Marty Levick